THE COMPLETE PIANO PLAYER GREAT CLASSICAL THEMES

Arranged by Kenneth Baker

Wise Publications
London / New York / Paris / Sydney / Copenhagen / Madrid

Exclusive Distributors:
Music Sales Limited
8/9 Frith Street,
London W1V 5TZ,
England.
Music Sales Pty Limited
120 Rothschild Avenue,
Rosebery, NSW 2018,
Australia.

This book © Copyright 1993 by Wise Publications
Order No. AM90150
ISBN 0-7119-3212-3

Book design by Studio Twenty, London
Compiled by Peter Evans
Music arranged by Kenneth Baker
Music processed by MSS Studios

Your Guarantee of Quality
As publishers, we strive to produce every book to the
highest commercial standards.
The music has been freshly engraved and the book has been
carefully designed to minimise awkward page turns and to
make playing from it a real pleasure.
Particular care has been given to specifying acid-free,
neutral-sized paper made from pulps which have not been elemental chlorine bleached.
This pulp is from farmed sustainable forests and was produced
with special regard for the environment.
Throughout, the printing and binding have been planned to ensure a sturdy,
attractive publication which should give years of enjoyment.
If your copy fails to meet our high standards, please
inform us and we will gladly replace it.

Music Sales' complete catalogue lists thousands of titles and is free
from your local music shop, or direct from Music Sales Limited.
Please send a cheque/postal order for £1.50 for postage to:
Music Sales Limited, Newmarket Road, Bury St. Edmunds,
Suffolk IP33 3YB.

JUPITER
(from "The Planets Suite")
by Gustav Holst

ROSAMUNDE OVERTURE

by Franz Schubert

PASTORAL SYMPHONY

by Ludwig Van Beethoven

LAND OF HOPE AND GLORY

by Sir Edward Elgar

POLOVTSIAN DANCE

by Alexander Borodin

MELODY IN F

by Anton Rubinstein

ROMEO AND JULIET

by Peter Ilyich Tchaikovsky

NORWEGIAN DANCE

by Edvard Grieg

MY HEART AT THY SWEET VOICE
(from "Samson And Delilah")

by Camille Saint-Saëns

SYMPHONY NO. 1

by Johannes Brahms

THEME

by Niccolo Paganini

SWAN LAKE

by Peter Ilyich Tchaikovsky

THE SWAN
(from "The Carnival Of Animals")
by Camille Saint-Saëns

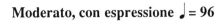

Moderato, con espressione ♩ = 96

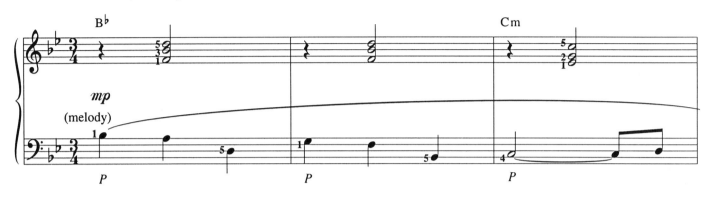

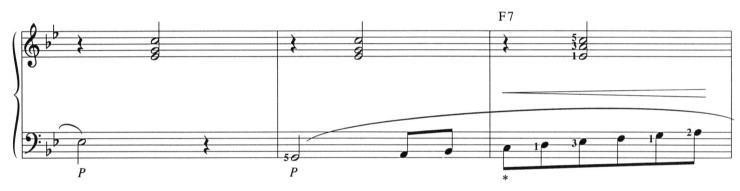

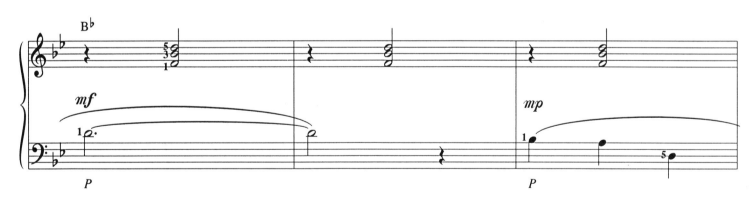

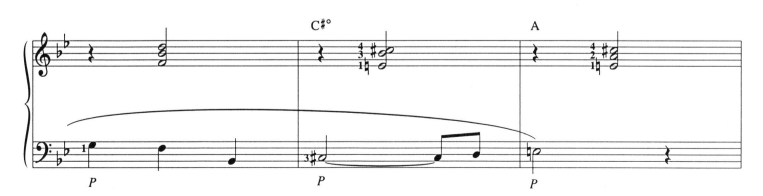

DANUBE WAVES

by Jan Ivanovici

THE UNFINISHED SYMPHONY

by Franz Schubert

GRAND MARCH
(from "Aida")
by Giuseppe Verdi

In the grand manner ♩ = 100

AVE MARIA

by Franz Schubert

ESPAÑA

by Emmanuel Chabrier

THE FOUR SEASONS
by Antonio Vivaldi

1. SPRING

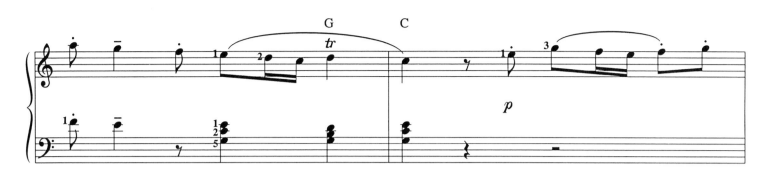

2. AUTUMN

Robustly ♩ = 126

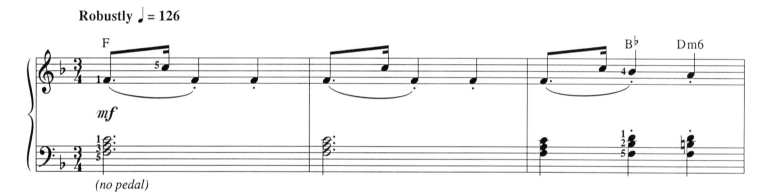

(no pedal)

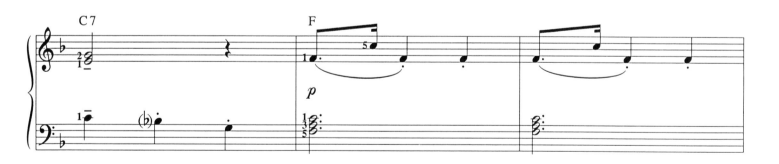

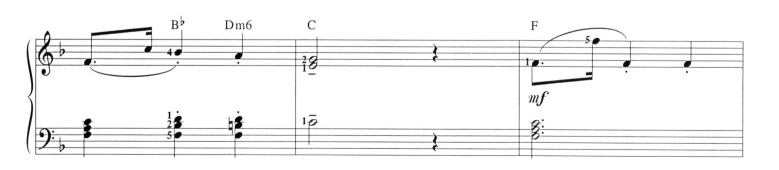

LARGO IN G

by George Frideric Handel

TRUMPET VOLUNTARY

by Jeremiah Clarke

THE MERRY WIVES OF WINDSOR
OVERTURE

by Karl Nicolai

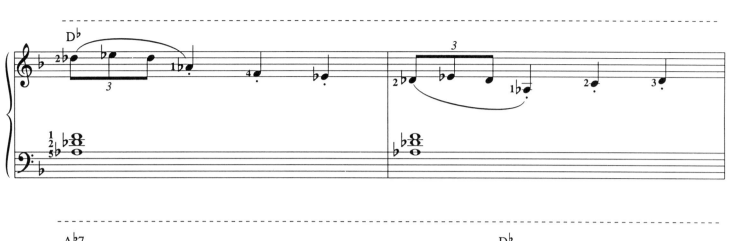

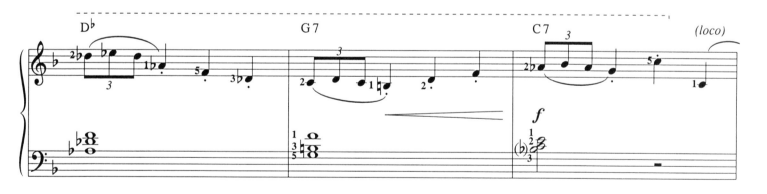

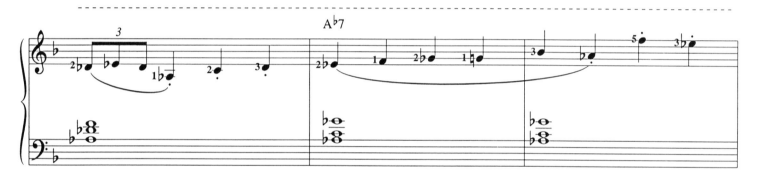

NESSUN DORMA
(from "Turandot")

by Giacomo Puccini

MEDITATION
(from "Thais")
by Jules Massenet

BERCEUSE

by Gabriel Fauré

EINE KLEINE NACHTMUSIK

by Wolfgang Amadeus Mozart

Printed in Great Britain by Printwise (Haverhill) Limited, Suffolk 12/99 (35936)